Original Designs by Dianne J. Hook

Deseret Book Company
Salt Lake City, Utah

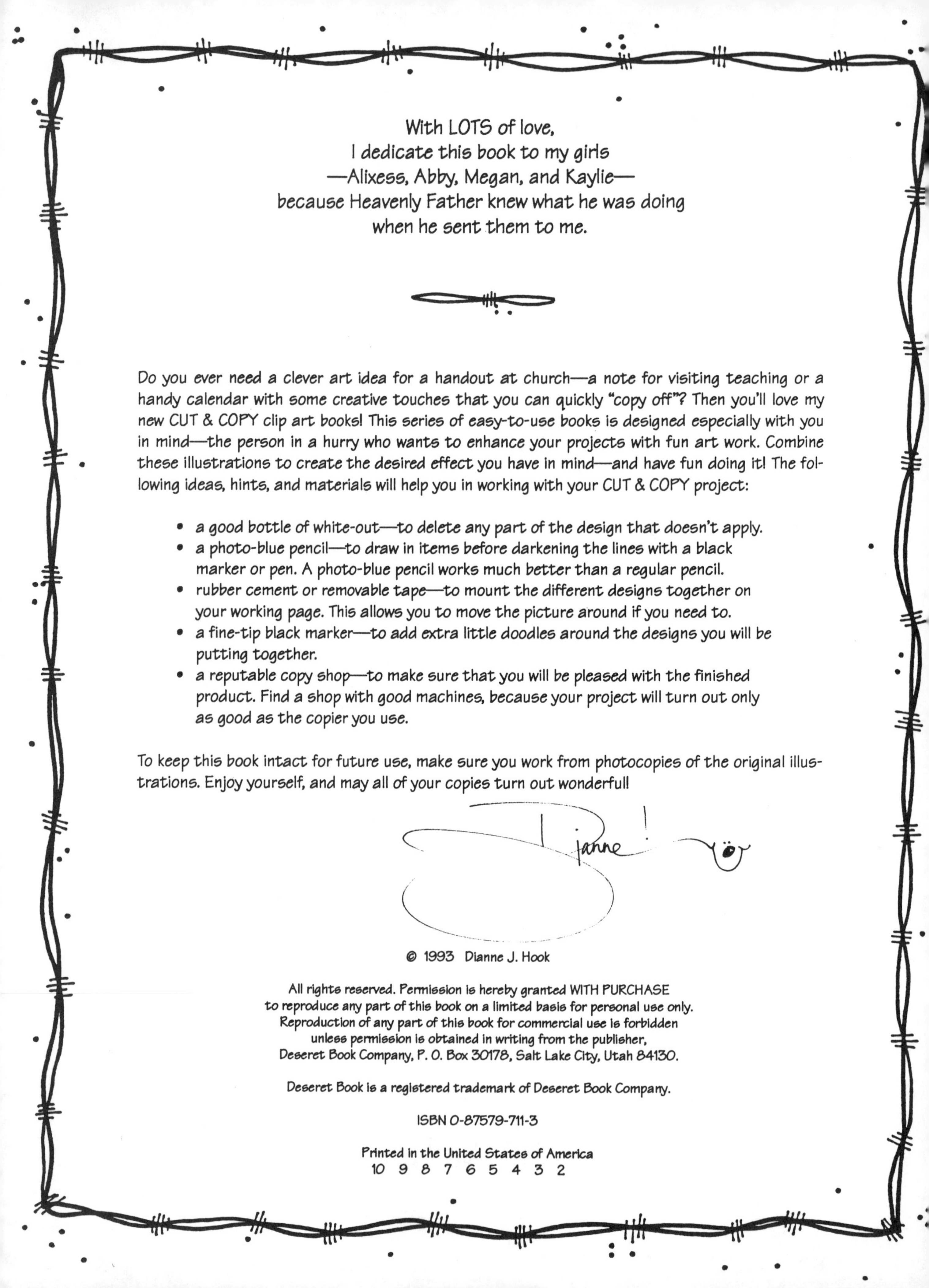

With LOTS of love,
I dedicate this book to my girls
—Alixess, Abby, Megan, and Kaylie—
because Heavenly Father knew what he was doing
when he sent them to me.

Do you ever need a clever art idea for a handout at church—a note for visiting teaching or a handy calendar with some creative touches that you can quickly "copy off"? Then you'll love my new CUT & COPY clip art books! This series of easy-to-use books is designed especially with you in mind—the person in a hurry who wants to enhance your projects with fun art work. Combine these illustrations to create the desired effect you have in mind—and have fun doing it! The following ideas, hints, and materials will help you in working with your CUT & COPY project:

- a good bottle of white-out—to delete any part of the design that doesn't apply.
- a photo-blue pencil—to draw in items before darkening the lines with a black marker or pen. A photo-blue pencil works much better than a regular pencil.
- rubber cement or removable tape—to mount the different designs together on your working page. This allows you to move the picture around if you need to.
- a fine-tip black marker—to add extra little doodles around the designs you will be putting together.
- a reputable copy shop—to make sure that you will be pleased with the finished product. Find a shop with good machines, because your project will turn out only as good as the copier you use.

To keep this book intact for future use, make sure you work from photocopies of the original illustrations. Enjoy yourself, and may all of your copies turn out wonderful!

© 1993 Dianne J. Hook

ISBN 0-87579-711-3

Printed in the United States of America
10 9 8 7 6 5 4 3 2

CUB SCOUTS

CUB SCOUTS

CUB SCOUTS

BOBCATS

BOBCAT

BOBCATS

BOBCATS

BOBCATS

WOLVES

WOLF

WOLVES

WOLVES

WOLVES

WEBELOS

WEBELO

WEBELOS

WEBELOS

WEBELOS

PACK MEETING
PACK MEETING

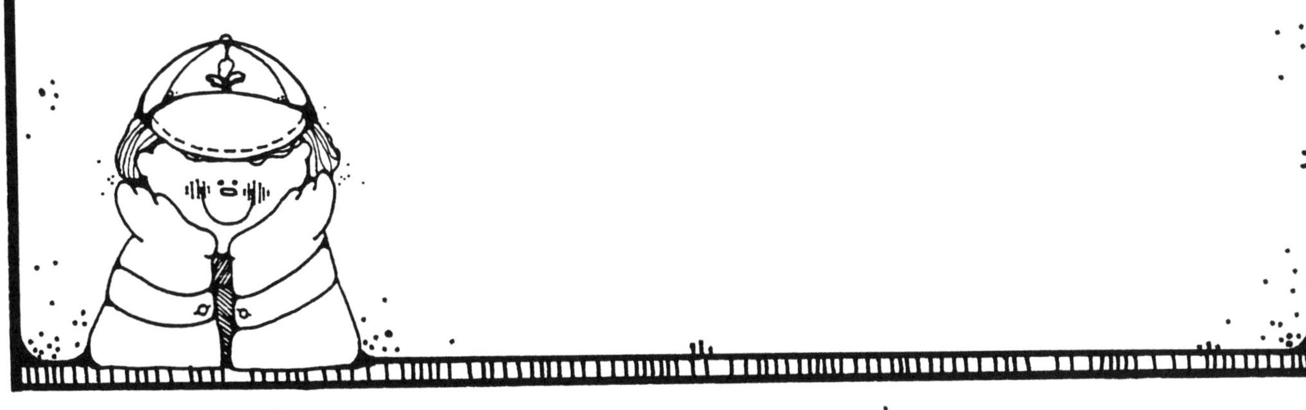

a reminder to parents....

PACK
MEETING

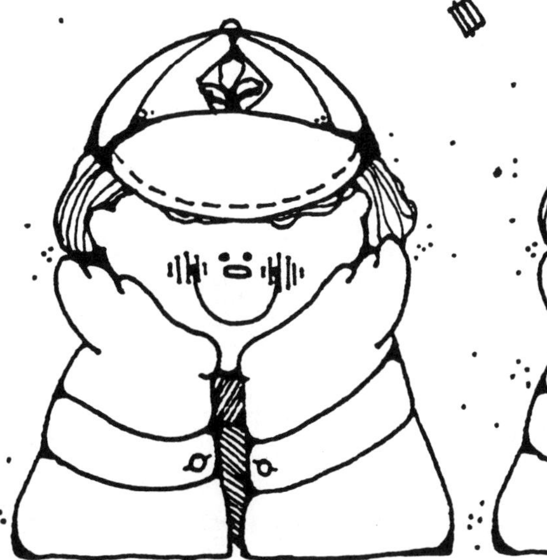

Blue & Gold Banquet

Blue & Gold Banquet

Pinewood Derby

Pinewood Derby

Medal
of Honor

SCOUTS

SCOUTS

SCOUTS

here's what's
happening
in SCOUTS

SCOUTS IN SERVICE
SCOUTS IN SERVICE
SCOUTS

THANK YOU!
from the whole troop!

DON'T FORGET!
This belongs to....
READ

SCOUTS
#4 TROOP

LOOK WHAT'S HOPPIN'...
SCOUT PARTY!
SCOUT PARTY!

Court of Honor

Date:

Time:

Place:

ON MY HONOR
This is presented to
for

FUND-RAISER
FUN!

COOL!

You're "OUT·OF·THIS WORLD" !

presented to

____

for

____

date _______________________ troop/den leader _______________

____

ATTENTION, SCOUTS!

camp out!
the great outdoors!

SIGN UP NOW!
CAMP
CAMP
CAMP

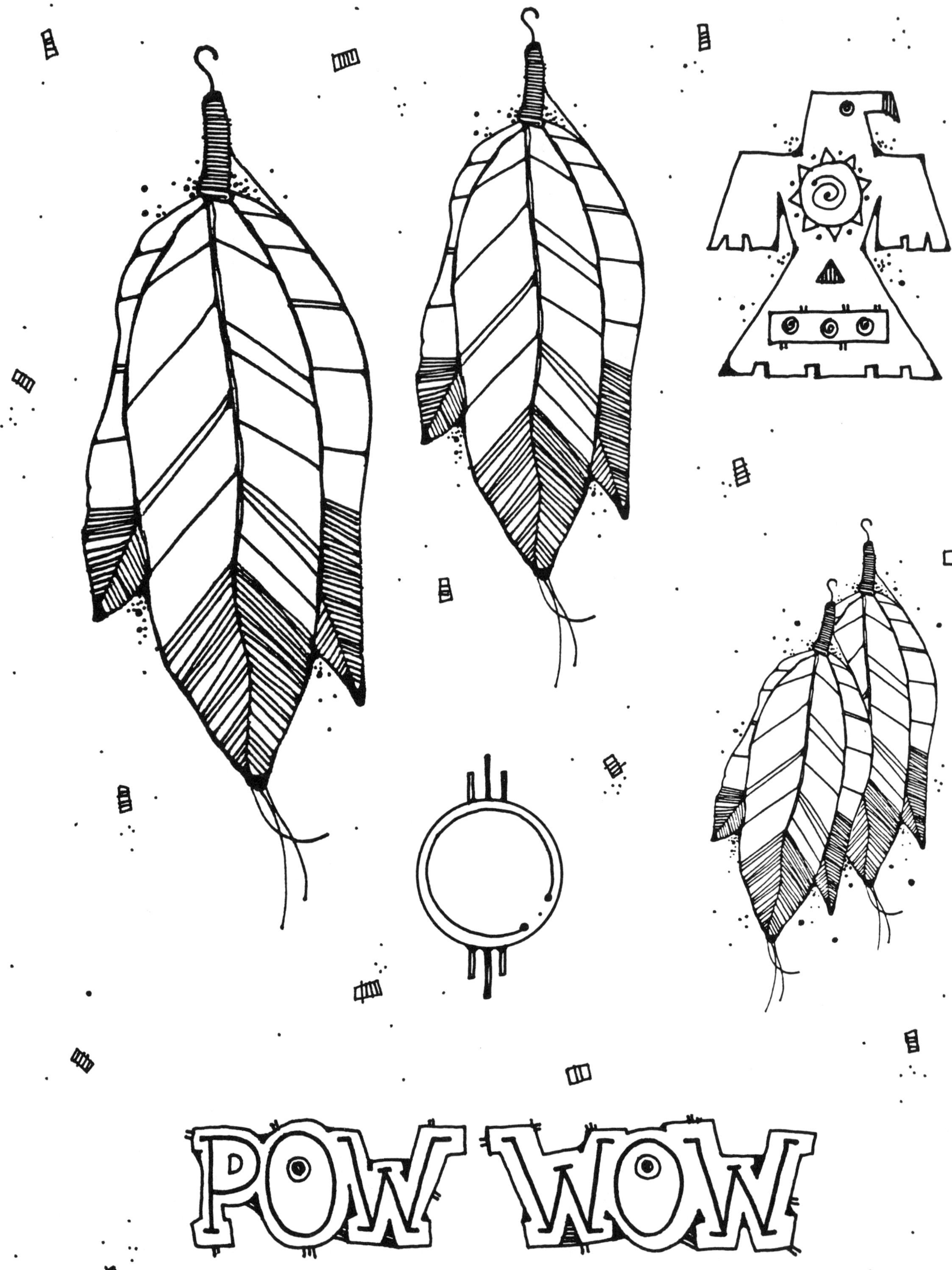

POW WOW

CAMPOREE!

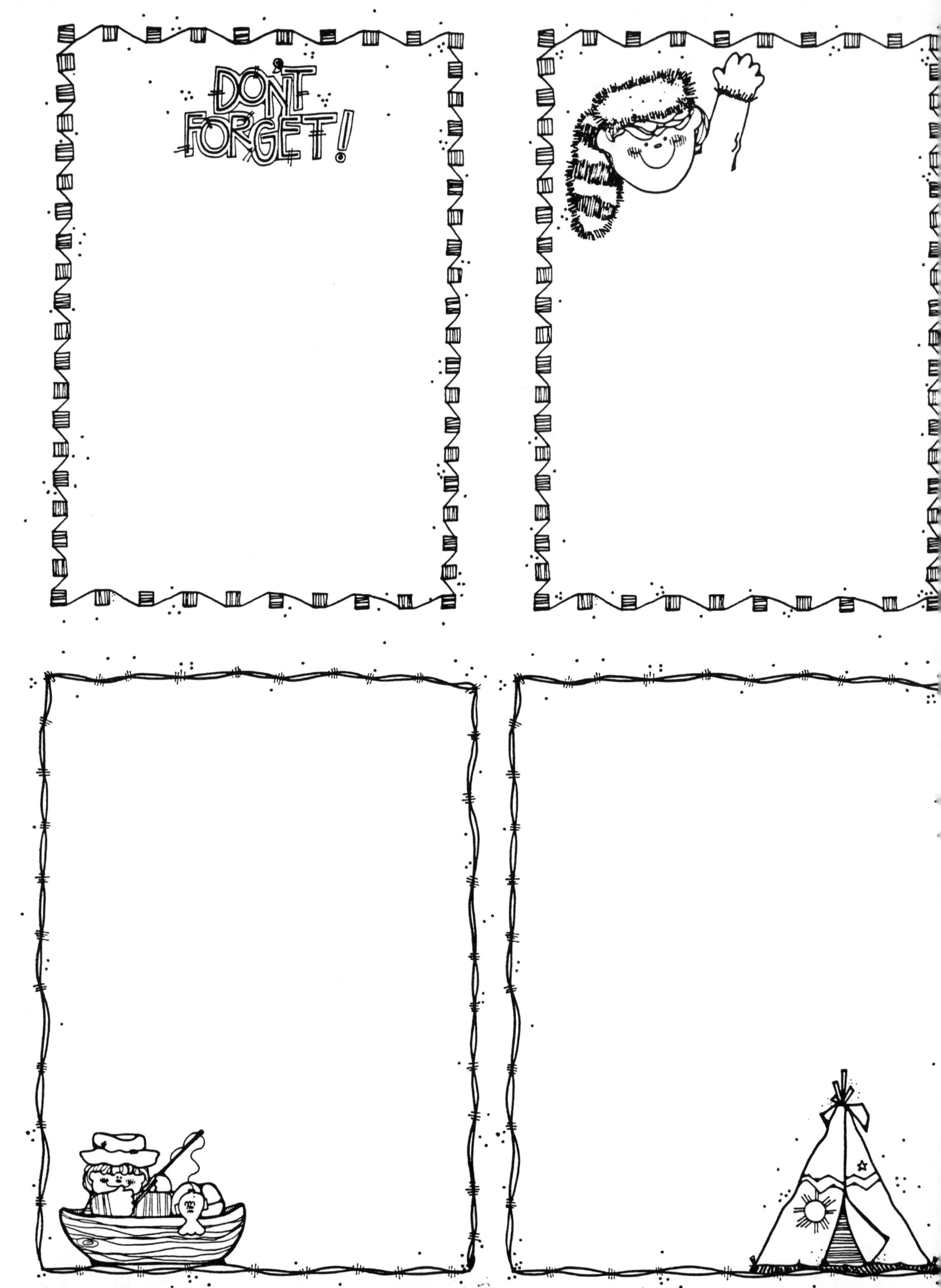
DON'T
FORGET!

DON'T MISS IT! 
FATHER & SON OUTING